CHRISTMAS CAROLS

for EASY GUITAR

Play the Melodies of 24 Holiday Favorites

ISBN 978-1-4234-1395-0

HAL•LEONARD®
CORPORATION

7777 W. BLUEMOUND RD. P.O. BOX 13819 MILWAUKEE, WI 53213

In Australia Contact:
Hal Leonard Australia Pty. Ltd.
4 Lentara Court
Cheltenham, Victoria, 3192 Australia
Email: ausadmin@halleonard.com

Visit Hal Leonard Online at
www.halleonard.com

Angels We Have Heard on High

Traditional French Carol
Translated by James Chadwick

Verse
Moderately

1. An - gels we have heard on high, sweet-ly sing-ing o'er the plains.
2. Shep - herds, why this ju - bi - lee? Why your joy-ous strains pro-long?
3., 4. *See additional lyrics*

And the moun-tains in re - ply, ech - o - ing their joy - ous strains.
What the glad - some tid - ings be which in - spire your heav - 'nly song?

Chorus

Glo - ri a in ex - cel - sis

De - o. Glo - ri - a

in ex - cel - sis De - o. o.

Additional Lyrics

3. Come to Bethlehem and see
Him whose birth the angels sing;
Come, adore on bended knee
Christ the Lord, the newborn King.

4. See within a manger laid
Jesus, Lord of heaven and earth!
Mary, Joseph, lend your aid,
With us sing our Savior's birth.

Away in a Manger

Traditional
Words by John T. McFarland (v.3)
Music by James R. Murray

Additional Lyrics

2. The cattle are lowing, the baby awakes,
   But little Lord Jesus, no crying He makes.
   I love Thee, Lord Jesus, look down from the sky
   And stay by my cradle till morning is nigh.

3. Be near me, Lord Jesus, I ask Thee to stay
   Close by me forever and love me, I pray.
   Bless all the dear children in Thy tender care
   And fit us for heaven to live with Thee there.

Carol of the Bells

Ukrainian Christmas Carol

Moderately fast

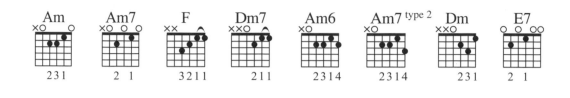

Hark to the bells, hark to the bells, tell - ing us all Je - sus is King!

Strong - ly they chime, sound with a rhyme, Christ - mas is here! Wel - come the King.

Hark to the bells, hark to the bells, this is the day, day of the King!

Peal out the news o'er hill and dale, and 'round the town tell - ing the tale.

Hark to the bells, hark to the bells, tell - ing us all Je - sus is King!

Come, one and all,— hap - pi - ly sing— songs of good will.— Oh, let them sing!

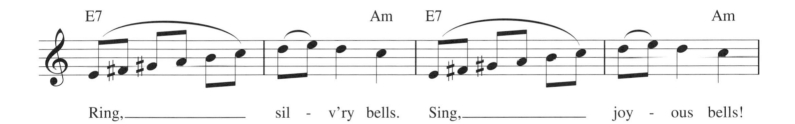

Ring,———— sil - v'ry bells. Sing,———— joy - ous bells!

Strong - ly they chime, sound with a rhyme, Christ - mas is here. Wel - come the King. Hark to the bells,

hark to the bells, tell - ing us all Je - sus is King! Ring! Ring!— bells.—

Deck the Hall

Traditional Welsh Carol

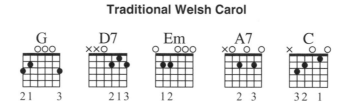

1. Deck the hall with boughs of hol-ly; fa, la, la, la, la, la, la, la, la.

2., 3. *See additional lyrics*

'Tis the sea-son to be jol-ly; fa, la, la, la, la, la, la, la, la.

Don we now our gay ap-par-el; fa, la, la, la, la, la, la, la, la.

Troll the an-cient yule-tide car-ol; fa, la, la, la, la, la, la, la, la. la, la, la.

Additional Lyrics

2. See the blazing yule before us;
Fa, la, la, la, la, la, la, la, la.
Strike the harp and join the chorus;
Fa, la, la, la, la, la, la, la, la.
Follow me in merry measure;
Fa, la, la, la, la, la, la, la, la.
While I tell of Yuletide treasure;
Fa, la, la, la, la, la, la, la, la.

3. Fast away the old year passes;
Fa, la, la, la, la, la, la, la, la.
Hail the new ye lads and lasses;
Fa, la, la, la, la, la, la, la, la.
Sing we joyous, all together;
Fa, la, la, la, la, la, la, la, la.
Heedless of the wind and weather;
Fa, la, la, la, la, la, la, la, la.

The First Noël

17th Century English Carol
Music from W. Sandy's Christmas Carols

Verse

Moderately slow

1. The first Noël, the an-gel did say, was to
2. - 5. *See additional lyrics*

cer-tain poor shep-herds in fields as they lay. In fields where

they lay keep-ing their sheep, on a cold win-ter's night that

Chorus

was so deep. No - ël, No - ël, No - ël, No -

ël, born is the King of Is - ra - el. 2. They el.

Additional Lyrics

2. They looked up and saw a star
   Shining in the east, beyond them far.
   And to the earth it gave great light
   And so it continued both day and night.

3. And by the light of that same star,
   Three wise men came from country far;
   To seek for a King was their intent,
   And to follow the star wherever it went.

4. This star drew nigh to the northwest,
   O'er Bethlehem it took its rest;
   And there it did both stop and say,
   Right over the place where Jesus lay.

5. Then entered in those wise men three,
   Full reverently upon their knee;
   And offered there in His presence,
   Their gold, and myrrh, and frankincense.

7

Go, Tell It on the Mountain

African-American Spiritual
Verses by John W. Work, Jr.

Additional Lyrics

2. The shepherds feared and trembled
   When, lo! above the earth
   Rang out the angel chorus
   That hailed our Savior's birth.

3. Down in a lowly manger
   Our humble Christ was born.
   And God sent us salvation
   That blessed Christmas morn.

God Rest Ye Merry, Gentlemen

19th Century English Carol

Additional Lyrics

2. In Bethlehem, in Jewry,
   This blessed babe was born,
   And laid within a manger
   Upon this blessed morn
   That which His mother Mary
   Did nothing take in scorn.

3. From God, our Heav'nly Father,
   A blessed angel came,
   And unto certain shepherds
   Brought tidings of the same.
   How that in Bethlehem was born
   The Son of God by name.

Good King Wenceslas

Words by John M. Neale
Music from Piae Cantiones

Verse
Moderately

1. Good King Wen - ces - las looked out on the feast of Ste - phen;
2. - 5. *See additional lyrics*

when the snow lay 'round a - bout, deep and crisp and e - ven.

Bright-ly shone the moon that night, though the frost was cru - el; when a poor man

came in sight, gath-'ring win - ter fu - el. ing.

Additional Lyrics

2. "Hither page, and stand by me,
   If thou know'st it telling;
   Yonder peasant, who is he?
   Where and what his dwelling?"
   "Sire, he lives a good league hence,
   Underneath the mountain;
   Right against the forest fence,
   By Saint Agnes fountain."

3. "Bring me flesh, and bring me wine,
   Bring me pine-logs hither;
   Thou and I will see him dine,
   When we bear then thither."
   Page and monarch forth they went,
   Forth they went together;
   Through the rude winds wild lament,
   And the bitter weather.

4. "Sire, the night is darker now,
   And the wind blows stronger;
   Fails my heart, I know not how,
   I can go not longer."
   "Mark my footsteps, my good page,
   Tread thou in them boldly;
   Thou shalt find the winter's rage
   Freeze thy blood less coldly."

5. In his master's steps he trod,
   Where the snow lay dinted;
   Heat was in the very sod
   Which the saint has printed.
   Therefore, Christmas men, be sure,
   Wealth or rank possessing;
   Ye who now will bless the poor,
   Shall yourselves find blessing.

I Saw Three Ships

Traditional English Carol

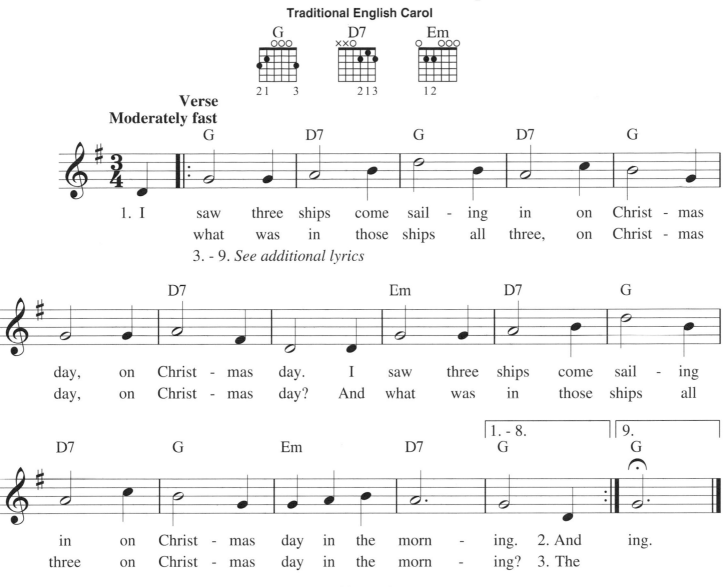

Additional Lyrics

3. The Virgin Mary and Christ were there on Christmas day, on Christmas day.
   The Virgin Mary and Christ were there on Christmas day in the morning.

4. Pray, whither sailed those ships all three on Christmas day, on Christmas day?
   Pray, whither sailed those ships all three on Christmas day in the morning?

5. Oh, they sailed into Bethlehem on Christmas day, on Christmas day.
   Oh, they sailed into Bethlehem on Christmas day in the morning.

6. And all the bells on earth shall ring on Christmas day, on Christmas day.
   And all the bells on earth shall ring on Christmas day in the morning.

7. And all the angels in heaven shall sing on Christmas day, on Christmas day.
   And all the angels in heaven shall sing on Christmas day in the morning.

8. And all the souls on earth shall sing on Christmas day, on Christmas day.
   And all the souls on earth shall sing on Christmas day in the morning.

9. Then let us all rejoice again on Christmas day, on Christmas day.
   Then let us all rejoice again on Christmas day in the morning.

Hark! The Herald Angels Sing

Words by Charles Wesley
Altered by George Whitefield
Music by Felix Mendelssohn-Bartholdy

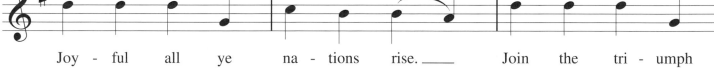

Additional Lyrics

2. Christ, by highest heav' adored, Christ, the everlasting Lord;
   Late in time behold Him come, offspring of the virgin's womb.
   Veil'd in flesh the Godhead see. Hail th'Incarnate Deity.
   Pleased as man with man to dwell, Jesus our Emmanuel!
   Hark! The herald angels sing, "Glory to the newborn King!"

3. Hail, the heav'n born Prince of Peace! Hail, the Son of Righteousness!
   Light and life to all He brings, ris'n with healing in His wings.
   Mild He lays His glory by. Born that man no more may die.
   Born to raise the sons of earth, born to give them second birth.
   Hark! The herald angels sing, "Glory to the newborn King!"

It Came Upon the Midnight Clear

Words by Edmund H. Sears
Traditional English Melody
Adapted by Arthur Sullivan

Jolly Old St. Nicholas

Traditional 19th Century American Carol

Verse
Moderately fast

1. Jol - ly old Saint Nich - o - las, lean your ear this way.
2., 3. *See additional lyrics*

Don't you tell a sin - gle soul what I'm going to say.

Christ - mas Eve is com - ing soon, now, you dear old man,

whis - per what you'll bring to me; tell me if you can. best.

Additional Lyrics

2. When the clock is striking twelve, when I'm fast asleep,
   Down the chimney broad and black, with your pack you'll creep.
   All the stockings you will find hanging in a row.
   Mine will be the shortest one, you'll be sure to know.

3. Johnny wants a pair of skates; Suzy wants a sled.
   Nellie wants a picture book, yellow, blue and red.
   Now I think I'll leave to you what to give the rest.
   Choose for me, dear Santa Claus, you will know the best.

Jingle Bells

Words and Music by J. Pierpont

Additional Lyrics

2. A day or two ago, I thought I'd take a ride,
   And soon Miss Fannie Bright was sitting by my side.
   The horse was lean and lank,
   Misfortune seemed his lot.
   He got into a drifted bank and we, we got upshot! Oh!

3. Now the ground is white, go it while you're young.
   Take the girls tonight and sing this sleighing song.
   Just get a bobtail bay,
   Two-forty for his speed.
   Then hitch him to an open sleigh and crack, you'll take the lead! Oh!

Joy to the World

Words by Isaac Watts
Music by George Frideric Handel

Additional Lyrics

3. No more let sin and sorrow grow,
Nor thorns infest the ground.
He comes to make His blessings flow
Far as the curse is found,
Far as the curse is found,
Far as, far as the curse is found.

4. He rules the world with truth and grace,
And makes the nations prove
The glories of His righteousness,
And wonders of His love,
And wonders of His love,
And wonders, wonders of His love.

O Christmas Tree

Traditional German Carol

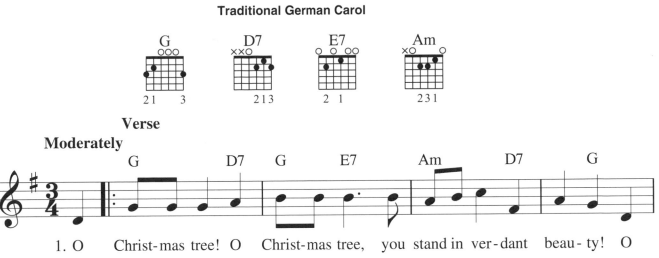

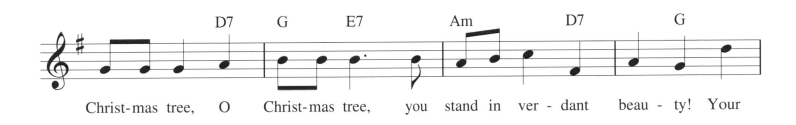

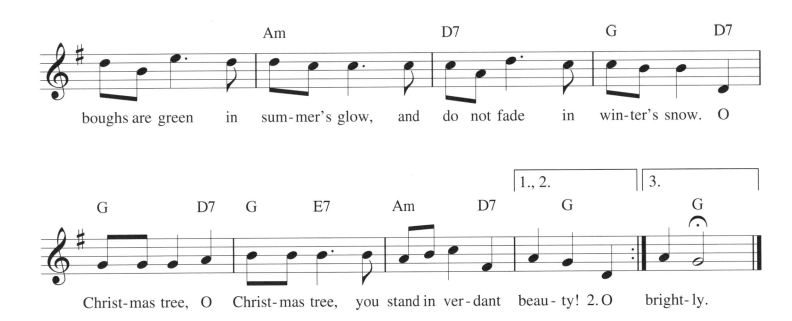

Additional Lyrics

2. O Christmas tree! O Christmas tree,
   Much pleasure doth thou bring me!
   O Christmas tree! O Christmas tree,
   Much pleasure does thou bring me!
   For every year the Christmas tree
   Brings to us all both joy and glee.
   O Christmas tree! O Christmas tree,
   Much pleasure doth thou bring me!

3. O Christmas tree! O Christmas tree,
   Thy candles shine out brightly!
   O Christmas tree, O Christmas tree,
   Thy candles shine out brightly!
   Each bough doth hold its tiny light
   That makes each toy to sparkle bright.
   O Christmas tree, O Christmas tree,
   Thy candles shine out brightly.

O Come, All Ye Faithful
(Adeste Fideles)

Words and Music by John Francis Wade
Latin Words translated by Frederick Oakeley

O Come, O Come Immanuel

Plainsong, 13th Century
Words translated by John M. Neale and Henry S. Coffin

Verse
Moderately

1. O come, O come, Im-man-u-el, and ran-som cap-tive
2., 3. *See additional lyrics*

Is-ra-el, that mourns in lone-ly ex-ile

here un-til the Son of God _____ ap-pear. Re-

Chorus

joice, re-joice! Im-man-u-el shall

come to thee, O Is-ra-el. 2. O el.

Additional Lyrics

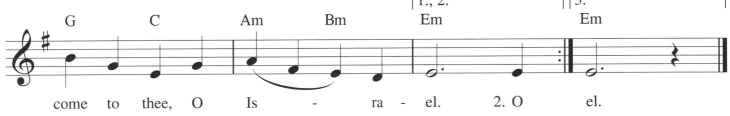

2. O come, Thou Wisdom from on high,
And order all things far and nigh;
To us, the path of knowledge show
And cause us in her ways to go.

3. O come, Desire of nations, bind
All people in one heart and mind;
Bid envy, strife, and quarrel's cease;
Fill the whole world with heaven's peace.

O Little Town of Bethlehem

Words by Phillips Brooks
Music by Lewis H. Redner

Silent Night

Words by Joseph Mohr
Translated by John F. Young
Music by Franz X. Gruber

Additional Lyrics

2. Silent night, holy night!
   Shepherds quake at the sight.
   Glories stream from heaven afar.
   Heavenly hosts sing Alleluia.
   Christ the Savior is born!
   Christ the Savior is born!

3. Silent night, holy night!
   Son of God, love's pure light.
   Radiant beams from thy holy face
   With the dawn of redeeming grace,
   Jesus Lord at Thy birth.
   Jesus Lord at Thy birth.

Up on the Housetop

Words and Music by B.R. Handy

Additional Lyrics

2. First comes the stocking of little Nell,
Oh, dear Santa, fill it well.
Give her a dollie that laughs and cries,
One that will open and shut her eyes.

3. Next comes the stocking of little Will,
Oh, just see what a glorious fill!
Here is a hammer and lots of tacks,
Also a ball and a whip that cracks.

We Wish You a Merry Christmas

Traditional English Folksong

We Three Kings of Orient Are

Words and Music by John H. Hopkins, Jr.

Verse

Moderately fast

1. We three Kings of Or - i - ent are
2. Born a King on Beth - le - hem plain,
3., 4., 5. *See additional lyrics*

bear - ing gifts we tra - verse a - far.
gold I bring to crown him a - gain.

Field and foun - tain, moor and moun - tain,
King for - ev - er, ceas - ing nev - er,

fol - low - ing yon - der star.
o - ver us all to reign.

O _____

Chorus

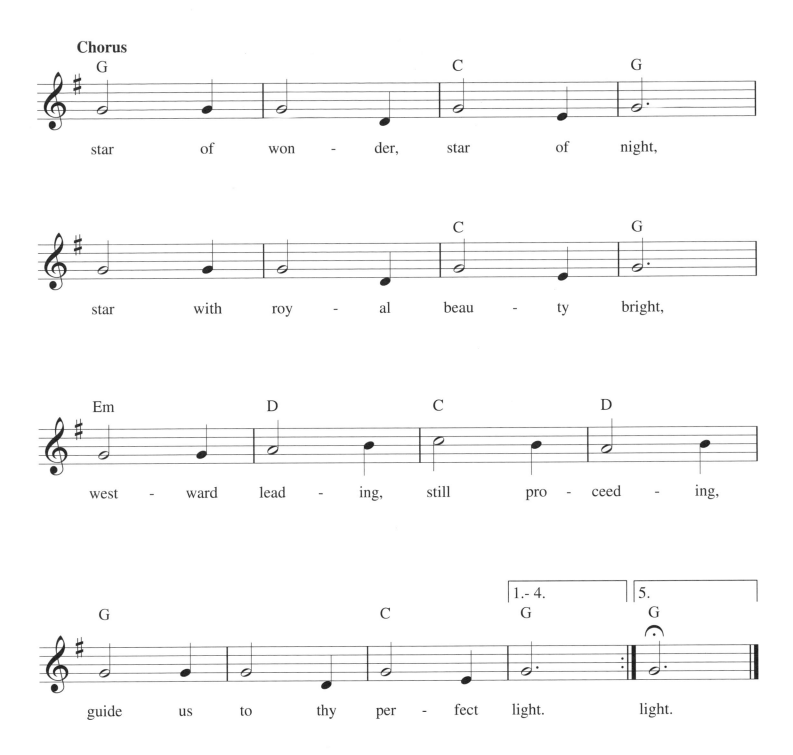

star of won - der, star of night,

star with roy - al beau - ty bright,

west - ward lead - ing, still pro - ceed - ing,

guide us to thy per - fect light. light.

Additional Lyrics

3. Frankincense to offer have I;
   Incense owns a Deity nigh;
   Prayer and praising, all men raising,
   Worship Him, God most high.

4. Myrrh us mine: it's bitter perfume
   Breathes a life of gathering gloom:
   Sorrowing, sighing, bleeding, dying;
   Sealed in the stone-cold tomb.

5. Glorious now, behold Him arise,
   King and God, and Sacrifice!
   Heav'n sings alleluia,
   Alleluia the earth replies:

What Child Is This?

Words by William C. Dix
16th Century English Melody

Verse
Moderately slow

1. What Child is this, ___ who, laid to rest, ___ on
2., 3. *See additional lyrics*

Ma - ry's lap ___ is sleep - ing? Whom

an - gels greet ___ with an - thems sweet ___ while

shep - herds watch ___ are keep - ing?

Chorus

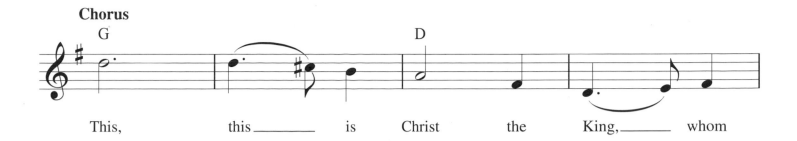

This,   this _____ is Christ the King, _____ whom

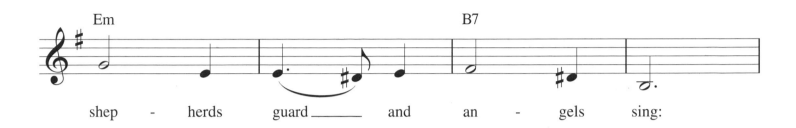

shep - herds guard _____ and an - gels sing:

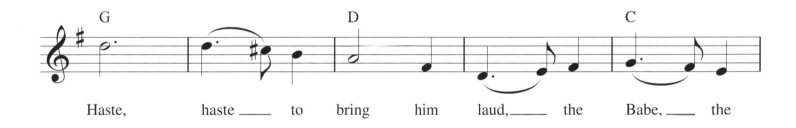

Haste,   haste ____ to bring him laud, ____ the Babe, ____ the

Son ____ of Ma - ry.   2. Why Ma - ry.

Additional Lyrics

2. Why lies He in such mean estate
   Where ox and ass are feeding?
   Good Christian, fear, for sinners here
   The silent word is pleading.

3. So bring Him incense, gold and myrrh.
   Come, peasant King, to own Him.
   The King of Kings salvation brings,
   Let loving hearts enthrone Him.

CHRISTMAS COLLECTIONS
FROM HAL LEONARD
ALL BOOKS ARRANGED FOR PIANO, VOICE & GUITAR

THE BEST CHRISTMAS SONGS EVER

69 all-time favorites: Auld Lang Syne • Coventry Carol • Frosty the Snow Man • Happy Holiday • It Came Upon the Midnight Clear • O Holy Night • Rudolph the Red-Nosed Reindeer • Silver Bells • What Child Is This? • and many more.

00359130 ....$29.99

THE BIG BOOK OF CHRISTMAS SONGS

Over 120 all-time favorites and hard-to-find classics: As Each Happy Christmas • The Boar's Head Carol • Carol of the Bells • Deck the Halls • The Friendly Beasts • God Rest Ye Merry Gentlemen • Joy to the World • Masters in This Hall • O Holy Night • Story of the Shepherd • and more.

00311520 ....$22.99

CHRISTMAS SONGS – BUDGET BOOKS

100 holiday favorites: All I Want for Christmas Is You • Christmas Time Is Here • Feliz Navidad • Grandma Got Run Over by a Reindeer • I'll Be Home for Christmas • Last Christmas • O Holy Night • Please Come Home for Christmas • Rockin' Around the Christmas Tree • We Need a Little Christmas • What Child Is This? • and more.

00310887 ....$14.99

CHRISTMAS MOVIE SONGS

34 holiday hits from the big screen: All I Want for Christmas Is You • Believe • Christmas Vacation • Do You Want to Build a Snowman? • Frosty the Snow Man • Have Yourself a Merry Little Christmas • It's Beginning to Look like Christmas • Mele Kalikimaka • Rudolph the Red-Nosed Reindeer • Silver Bells • White Christmas • You're a Mean One, Mr. Grinch • and more.

00146961 ....$19.99

CHRISTMAS PIANO SONGS FOR DUMMIES®

56 favorites: Auld Lang Syne • Away in a Manger • Blue Christmas • The Christmas Song • Deck the Hall • I'll Be Home for Christmas • Jingle Bells • Joy to the World • My Favorite Things • Silent Night • more!

00311387 ....$19.95

CHRISTMAS POP STANDARDS

22 contemporary holiday hits, including: All I Want for Christmas Is You • Christmas Time Is Here • Little Saint Nick • Mary, Did You Know? • Merry Christmas, Darling • Santa Baby • Underneath the Tree • Where Are You Christmas? • and more.

00348998 ....$14.99

CHRISTMAS SING-ALONG

40 seasonal favorites: Away in a Manger • Christmas Time Is Here • Feliz Navidad • Happy Holiday • Jingle Bells • Mary, Did You Know? • O Come, All Ye Faithful • Rudolph the Red-Nosed Reindeer • Silent Night • White Christmas • and more. Includes online sing-along backing tracks.

00278176 Book/Online Audio $24.99

CHRISTMAS SONGS FOR KIDS

28 favorite songs of the season, including: Away in a Manger • Do You Want to Build a Snowman? • Here Comes Santa Claus (Right down Santa Claus Lane) • Mele Kalikimaka • Rudolph the Red-Nosed Reindeer • Santa Claus Is Comin' to Town • Silent Night • Somewhere in My Memory • and many more.

00311571 ....$12.99

100 CHRISTMAS CAROLS

Includes: Away in a Manger • Bring a Torch, Jeannette, Isabella • Coventry Carol • Deck the Hall • The First Noel • Go, Tell It on the Mountain • I Heard the Bells on Christmas Day • Joy to the World • O Come, All Ye Faithful (Adeste Fideles) • Silent Night • Sing We Now of Christmas • and more.

00310897 ....$19.99

100 MOST BEAUTIFUL CHRISTMAS SONGS

Includes: Angels We Have Heard on High • Baby, It's Cold Outside • Christmas Time Is Here • Do You Hear What I Hear • Grown-Up Christmas List • Happy Xmas (War Is Over) • I'll Be Home for Christmas • The Little Drummer Boy • Mary, Did You Know? • O Holy Night • White Christmas • Winter Wonderland • and more.

00237285 ....$24.99

POPULAR CHRISTMAS SHEET MUSIC: 1980-2017

40 recent seasonal favorites: All I Want for Christmas Is You • Because It's Christmas (For All the Children) • Breath of Heaven (Mary's Song) • Christmas Lights • The Christmas Shoes • The Gift • Grown-Up Christmas List • Last Christmas • Santa Tell Me • Snowman • Where Are You Christmas? • Wrapped in Red • and more.

00278089 ....$17.99

A SENTIMENTAL CHRISTMAS BOOK

27 beloved Christmas favorites, including: The Christmas Shoes • The Christmas Song (Chestnuts Roasting on an Open Fire) • Christmas Time Is Here • Grown-Up Christmas List • Have Yourself a Merry Little Christmas • I'll Be Home for Christmas • Somewhere in My Memory • Where Are You Christmas? • and more.

00236830 ....$14.99

ULTIMATE CHRISTMAS

100 seasonal favorites: Auld Lang Syne • Bring a Torch, Jeannette, Isabella • Carol of the Bells • The Chipmunk Song • Christmas Time Is Here • The First Noel • Frosty the Snow Man • Gesù Bambino • Happy Holiday • Happy Xmas (War Is Over) • Jingle-Bell Rock • Pretty Paper • Silver Bells • Suzy Snowflake • and more.

00361399 ....$24.99

A VERY MERRY CHRISTMAS

39 familiar favorites: Blue Christmas • Feliz Navidad • Happy Xmas (War Is Over) • I'll Be Home for Christmas • Jingle-Bell Rock • Please Come Home for Christmas • Rockin' Around the Christmas Tree • Santa, Bring My Baby Back (To Me) • Sleigh Ride • White Christmas • and more.

00310536 ....$14.99

HAL•LEONARD®

**Complete contents listings available online at
www.halleonard.com**

PRICES, CONTENTS, AND AVAILABILITY SUBJECT
TO CHANGE WITHOUT NOTICE.

0621
302